Horses!

Horse Shows

Susan H. Gray

Cavendish Square

New York

Published in 2014 by Cavendish Square Publishing, LLC
303 Park Avenue South, Suite 1247, New York, NY 10010

Website: cavendishsq.com

This publication represents the opinions and views of the author based on his or her personal experience, knowledge, and research. The information in this book serves as a general guide only. The author and publisher have used their best efforts in preparing this book and disclaim liability rising directly or indirectly from the use and application of this book.

CPSIA Compliance Information: Batch #WS13CSQ

All websites were available and accurate when this book was sent to press.

Library of Congress Cataloging-in-Publication Data
Gray, Susan Heinrichs.
Horse Shows / Susan H. Gray
      p. cm. — (Horses!)
Includes bibliographical references and index.
Summary: "Provides comprehensive information on the history of horse shows, types of shows, and how to get started"—Provided by publisher.
ISBN 978-1-60870-838-3 (hardcover)   ISBN 978-1-62712-088-3 (paperback)   978-1-60870-831-4 (ebook)
1. Horse shows—Juvenile literature. I. Title. II. Series.
SF294.7.G73 2013
798.2 4—dc23
2011012788

Editor: Christine Florie
Art Director: Anahid Hamparian
Series Designer: Virginia Pope

Expert reader: Cathy Herbert, former director of publications, American Horse Shows Association

Photo research by Marybeth Kavanagh

Cover photo by The Irish Image Collection/SuperStock

The photographs in this book are used by permission and through the courtesy of: *Corbis*: Paul Roberts/OFFSIDE, 4; Larry W. Smith/epa, 20; *The Image Works*: Antman Archives, 7; Balean/TopFoto, 9; *North Wind Picture Archives*: 8; *Alamy*: Dennis MacDonald, 10; Jim West, 12; SportsAction, 14; worldinmyeyes.pl, 22; Rick Strange, 34; The Photolibrary Wales, 36; Ron Buskirk, 40; *Getty Images*: Mario Villafuerte, 13; Tim Graham, 15; Tim Platt Photography, 29; Richard A. Lipski/The Washington Post, 39; *AP Photo*: Amy Sancetta, 16; Scanpix Sweden, Henrik Montgomery, 19; *SuperStock*: NaturePL, 21; Cusp, 26; Robert Harding Picture Library, 30; *Newscom*: Mark Cornelison/MCT, 24

Printed in the United States of America

Contents

One

Horse Shows through the Years

Horse shows are exciting and fun events. They are exhibitions in which riders show off their horses and prove how well they ride and handle them. Shows also give horses a chance to display their skills, such as jumping, pulling carriages, or herding cows. But that is not all. These shows are competitions. They test how well riders deal with problems and handle pressure. They also test how well horses respond to their riders' signals, such as slight leg movements or changes in hand position.

Crowds love to watch competitors in colorful outfits and horses with shiny coats. And judges like to see riders who communicate well with their animals. They watch to see if the riders are confident and skilled. They look at how gracefully the horses do specific movements. Judges keep score based on how well the horses and riders perform. The pair with the best scores usually wins ribbons or trophies.

← Horse shows have been taking place since the days of ancient Greece. Today, people still enjoy them.

Many horse shows are quite small. They might be held at local barns, where competitors are there mostly to have fun. Others can be quite large. Big shows might have more than a hundred different events. They might go on for days, with hundreds of horses and riders competing. But long ago, horse shows were much simpler affairs.

Some Wild Rides

More than 2,500 years ago, people in Greece entered their horses in the Olympics. They competed in **chariot** races and riding contests. Winners did not receive trophies. Instead, they won crowns made from the branches of olive trees. Riders became famous and were hailed as heroes in their hometowns.

An Early Horse Trainer

Xenophon (ZEN-uh-fun) was a horse lover who lived in ancient Greece. In his book *On Horsemanship*, he described everything he knew about buying, training, and riding horses. Xenophon explained how to teach horses to walk in a "grand style." He wrote that a horse in a parade should be a "high stepper and showy." Perhaps Xenophon was one of the first horse-show trainers!

Chariot races were a featured event in the ancient Olympic Games in Greece.

Over the years, different horse competitions developed. Long ago, people in England and France held **jousting** contests where knights in armor rode large, sturdy horses. Using **lances**, they tried to knock other knights from their **steeds**. Crowds came to cheer for their favorite knights. Great shouts rose up each time a knight tumbled from his horse.

During the middle ages, jousting was a way for knights to practice horsemanship skills and use of a lance.

These contests were fun and exciting for the audiences, but horses and riders often got hurt.

Making Improvements

By the late 1800s, horse competitions were much safer and more organized. Knights no longer competed in jousting contests. Instead, shows in England featured jumping events. At shows in Ireland, the best hunting horses earned prizes. And shows in the United States drew attention to carriage horses.

Today, horse shows take place in almost every country in the world. In many cities, certain shows are held year after year. Some shows allow only one **breed**, or type of horse, to compete. For instance, a huge show in Arizona is just for Arabian horses. An Oklahoma show allows only Morgan horses. Many other shows permit all types of horses or ponies to enter.

Steeplechase horse racing involves racing and jumping over rough terrain that includes stone walls, water, and fences.

Two

A Show for Every Horse and Rider

Today, it's unlikely that you will see chariot races or jousting at a horse show. But you might watch **endurance riding**, where the horse and rider travel long distances. Or you might see contests in which riders and horses are dressed in costumes. People who run horse shows have come up with hundreds of ways for horses and riders to compete.

Every show is divided into different categories called classes. Riders and horses within the same class compete with each other. One class might include only female horses of a certain breed or age, such as one-year-old quarter horse fillies. Another class might be just for riders who are ten to twelve years old. Yet other classes could be for ponies pulling carts or horses that perform fancy steps.

Classes might also include horses shown in hand or horses under saddle. When a person leads an unmounted horse around an arena, he or she is

← This girl competes in the "in hand" class as she leads her horse around the arena.

11

Judging the Riders

In **equitation** classes, judges grade the riders, not the horses. They look closely at each rider's position and balance and how effortlessly he or she controls the horse.

Riders signal their horses with very slight movements. They might gently nudge the horse with their legs or shift their weight in the saddle. In some classes, riders wear white gloves that contrast with their horses' colors. Judges can easily see if the riders' hand signals are too obvious.

showing the horse in hand. Horses with riders are competing under saddle. With hundreds of shows and classes around, there is certainly something for every horse and rider.

Western and English Classes

In different parts of the world, horse lovers have their own favorite classes. For instance, in North America, western classes are popular. In western

classes, riders use the kind of **tack**, or equipment, that cowboys use. This includes a large, sturdy saddle with a raised knob called the horn, used in roping. Western riders hold their **reins** in one hand, just like cowboys who need to rope with the other hand. In shows, competitors wear jeans, cowboy

The Rodeo

Is the rodeo a horse show? Not really. Rodeo riders do show how well they and their horses perform. They compete for prizes. But in a rodeo, competitors might also ride enormous bulls, and children might rope goats or ride sheep.

Cowboys developed the rodeo for ranch horses in the 1800s. Back then, cowboys in Mexico, Canada, and the United States went on long, tiring cattle drives. They drove cattle herds from ranches to **cow towns**, where the cattle were sold. While in town, the cowboys had fun by showing off their riding and roping skills. Over time, these get-togethers became more organized. Today, rodeos are popular mainly in North America. Many cities have junior rodeos just for kids.

boots, chaps, cowboy hats, and colorful long-sleeved shirts or jackets.

English riding is also popular in many parts of the world. An English-style rider uses a small, light saddle without a horn. This saddle gives the rider more contact with the horse. English riders use both hands to hold the reins. In horse shows, the riders wear tall boots, snug-fitting pants, a solid-color jacket, gloves, a shirt with a white collar and cuffs, and a helmet or top hat.

Shows in Other Countries

Australian shows often include tent-pegging competitions. In tent pegging, riders carry lances and their horses gallop toward pegs in the ground. As the horses pass by, riders jab the pegs with their lances and scoop them up.

Western horse shows are competitions where horses display their response to their rider, their manner, and their disposition.

Sometimes riders miss the pegs completely. Judges give low scores to those riders.

Shows just for Arabian horses are especially popular in the Middle East. In this region of the world, people have raised Arabians for many years. These animals are energetic and sturdy, and they have big lungs. Arabians can withstand long journeys through hot, dry areas. Shows in Saudi Arabia often include rides through the desert to prove how tough the horses are.

English-style riding orig... good way to learn how t... control the movement o...

Three

The Official Disciplines

While modern-day horse shows offer many different classes, some shows focus on seven official **disciplines**. The international organization Fédération Equestre Internationale (FEI) has selected seven events that are most popular around the world. These seven disciplines are jumping, dressage, endurance, driving, reining, eventing, and vaulting. FEI officials created the rules that riders and horses must follow when competing in these disciplines. Many of the rules involve the safety and health of the horses.

Jumping

In a jumping competition, a horse and rider follow a course in a ring with ten to thirteen **obstacles**. The obstacles might include fences, walls, hedges, and ponds. Riders guide their horses to jump them in a specific order.

← Jumping is one of the seven disciplines in horse shows.

The Four Gaits

Horse-show judges often ask riders to have their horses perform different gaits. The gaits are the different manners in which a horse moves forward. There are four basic gaits: walk, trot, canter, and gallop.

The walk is a slow gait in which the horse lifts each foot separately. The trot is a little faster, and the legs move in diagonal pairs. The canter, a three-beat gait, is faster still, and the gallop is the fastest of all.

Judges watch to see how well the horses and riders work together to clear each obstacle. Horses receive penalties if they land in a pond, refuse to jump, or jump the obstacles in the wrong order. Any horse or rider who falls is disqualified. The fastest horse with the fewest penalties wins.

Dressage

Dressage is a discipline that teaches the horse to be obedient and graceful. The horse learns to respond to very slight, gentle movements of the rider's hands, legs, seat, and upper body. The rider's guidance should be so subtle that the judges do not even notice the cues.

A horse and rider compete in a dressage competition.

Dressage competitions take place in arenas. At the start of the competition, the horse and rider enter and stop at the center of the arena. Judges evaluate whether the horse stands perfectly square and at attention. They also note whether the rider sits up straight. In dressage, both the horse and the rider get a score.

Next, with its rider's guidance, the horse walks, trots, and canters for the judges. It may show its gaits in figure-eight patterns, in circles, or along S-shaped paths. Judges score the horses and riders on how gracefully they perform and how smoothly they work together.

Dressage competitions often include performances to music. In freestyle, one horse and rider perform. In other displays, two or four horses and their riders perform together.

Dressage judges like to see horses and riders that are well turned out, meaning that they look great. A nicely turned-out horse has a shiny coat. His mane is braided, and his hooves are polished. Each rider should be neatly dressed in an English riding outfit.

Endurance

An endurance competition tests how well horses can travel over long distances. Competitions usually involve one-day rides of up to 100 miles. The horses travel through fields and forests, over roads, across streams, and up and down hills.

Each course is divided into sections called phases. At the end of each phase, veterinarians inspect the horses. They check to see how tired the horses are, if their heart rates are too high, if they are breathing too hard, or if they are overheating. No horse and rider can continue until the vet says it is okay.

Throughout the competition, riders count on their support crews for help. On hot days, support crews bring water to splash over the horses. They also bring cool drinks for the riders.

A horse gets watered down during the 2010 Endurance Championship of the World Equestrian Games in Lexington, Kentucky.

Driving

In driving each horse pulls a carriage or cart with a driver. Carriages may be pulled by one, two, or four horses or ponies. In training, these horses learn to follow the drivers' voice commands and rein movements. They also learn to respond to gentle touches with a whip.

Driving competitions usually include three parts: dressage, marathon, and obstacles called cones. In the dressage section, horses walk or trot as they pull their carriages in a circle or a straight line. While they make turns and stops, judges watch how accurately they perform a pattern. In the marathon section, the horses pull their carriages cross-country. They show how well they deal with streams, sharp turns, and hills. Finally, the competitors finish up with the cones section. Here, the drivers guide their horses through a narrow track. Along the track are cones, each with a ball balanced on top. If a horse or carriage knocks off a ball, the team loses points.

One of the three parts of a driving competition is marathon. One of its requirements is to drive a horse through a stream.

Reining

Reining is a western discipline that shows off the skills of a ranch horse. Ranchers use them to herd cattle into pens and to separate single cows from the group. These horses must be able to respond to very light commands. The horses respond to the feeling of the reins on the neck, nudges of the riders' legs and feet, and spoken commands.

The ranch horse has to stay alert. It must be able to break into a gallop, make sharp turns, stop quickly, and back up. During a reining competition, the horse must perform several moves. Two of the most exciting moves are the spin and the sliding stop. In the spin, the horse leaves one hind foot in the same spot while spinning in a circle. For the sliding stop, the horse begins with a bounding gait. At the rider's command, the horse suddenly locks his hind legs

A horse performs a sliding stop during a reining competition.

under his body and slides on his back feet. Both horse and rider must have excellent muscle control and balance to perform this well.

For reining events, riders wear western clothing. Some people like to catch the judge's eye with rhinestones on their belts. Others wear bright shirts that contrast with their horses' colors. Everyone wears cowboy hats.

Eventing

A combination of three disciplines, eventing shows skills in dressage, cross-country, and stadium jumping. This competition tests the horse's obedience, bravery, and agility. In eventing, the horse and rider must work together smoothly in every situation.

On the first day of the competition, dressage shows off the horse's grace and obedience in the arena. During day two, horses run cross-country. This thrilling event exhibits the animals' speed, jumping ability, and endurance on an outdoor course with several types of obstacles. On the third day, the horses and riders return to the arena for the stadium-jumping competition. This event proves the horse's agility while clearing a course of up to thirteen jumps.

Veterinarians check the horses every day to make sure they are fit to continue. Riders also make sure their horses are not getting tired. Riders may pull their horses out of the competition at any time.

Vaulting

The discipline that combines horsemanship with dance and gymnastics is called vaulting. In this sport, one or more people perform gymnastic feats atop a cantering horse. Guided by a person called the **longeur**, the horse canters in a wide circle. The longeur holds a long line attached to the horse. He or she makes sure the horse stays in the circle and does not speed up or slow down.

As the horse canters, one or more riders perform stunning routines. They may perform handstands or cartwheels. Two vaulters might take turns lifting each other into beautiful ballet poses.

Team Argentina performs their routine during the team freestyle vaulting competition at the 2010 World Equestrian Games in Lexington, Kentucky.

A vaulting horse must be very sturdy. It should have a wide back and strong legs. Its neck should be short and thick. The horse must also be very steady. While it canters, it carries a lot of constantly shifting weight on its back.

Vaulting is often performed to stirring music. Vaulters usually wear tights and leotards so they can move freely. People who compete in vaulting must be in excellent shape. They often take dance and gymnastic lessons to learn the different moves and poses.

Para-equestrian Events

Dressage and driving competitions often include classes for para-**equestrians**. Para-equestrians are riders who have disabilities. Some people think the prefix *para-* has to do with people who are paralyzed. However, this is not the case. *Para* is short for *parallel*, as this sport parallels, or runs alongside, other equestrian sports.

A doctor checks each para-equestrian before he or she competes. The doctor looks for good muscle strength, balance, and coordination. Para-equestrians can compete in horse shows only if their doctors approve.

Many countries have horse shows with para-equestrian events. The best athletes from these competitions go on to the Paralympics or the World Equestrian Games. Most para-equestrians compete in para-dressage or para-driving. However, para-jumping is also growing in popularity.

Four

Getting Started

How does someone get into a horse show? Is buying a horse the first step? Where do riders find out about shows? How do you know which class to compete in?

If you have not grown up around horses, you have plenty to learn. A training stable is a great place to start. Look in the telephone book or online to see if there is a horse-training stable near you. Ask **equine** veterinarians and people at feed or tack stores if they know of any good stables. Once you have some stables in mind, give them a call. Ask if you can come out for a tour.

Checking Things Out

A good stable will have clean stalls, healthy horses, and happy students. It will also have friendly trainers who care about the safety of their riders.

← A horse stable is a great place to learn about horses, riding, and shows.

Learning to Jump

Trainers have come up with many clever ways to teach horses to perform. To teach a horse to jump, a trainer starts with very easy moves. He or she has the horse step over poles lying on the ground. As soon as the horse is used to this, the trainer raises the poles a bit. Once the horse moves easily over this new height, the poles go up again.

The trainers should not mind if you want to watch a lesson or two. You should learn which disciplines they focus on and find out if they teach riders your age. You might also ask if the barn conducts shows. Find out as much as you can about the stable and trainers. You might have to look at two or three different stables before you find one that seems right for you.

At a good stable, you will learn much more than how to ride. You will learn about caring for a horse and grooming it. You'll find out how to bathe the horse, brush it, and care for its hooves. You will learn how to use the different pieces of riding equipment and tack up your horse.

You should also learn about horses' **temperaments**. You will get to know horses that are calm, energetic, easily bored, or eager to please. You will begin to see which type of horse matches you best. This is especially

At a horse stable, you will learn how to groom a horse.

important if you expect to own a horse one day. Far too many people buy horses that do not match their personalities.

During riding lessons, you will learn the proper way to mount and dismount. You will find out about the different gaits. You will learn how to use the reins and your knees,

Pony Clubs and 4-H

Many young riders want to do more than take lessons, so they join pony clubs or 4-H groups. In 4-H, children can learn much more than riding. They learn how to select a horse of their own. They also learn how to raise horses and keep them healthy.

Pony clubs are for children and young adults who share an interest in horses and ponies. Adult volunteers lead these clubs, and every club is different. At meetings, members may learn tips on horse care and riding safety. They might also learn the polite and proper behavior for shows. Pony clubs exist in towns all across the United States—even in Alaska.

hands, and heels to control the horse. You may start out with the horse on a long line so that you can practice balance exercises. You will also learn how to signal your horse to turn, slow down, speed up, jump, or perform other maneuvers.

Practice Shows

Many stables put on small horse shows just for their own students or other riders in the area. These give students a chance to practice before going to a more formal show. At these schooling shows, riders perform before a judge. The judge asks students to ride at a walk, trot, and canter. He or she might ask students to ride in a figure-eight pattern

An important part of riding lessons is to learn the right way to get on and off a horse.

or do some jumps. The judge scores each student and writes comments on his or her scorecard. Comments tell the riders what they are doing well and where they need to improve.

Small shows like this have several advantages. Riders learn how to ride before a judge. The entry fees are much lower than those at regular shows. And the horses are already at the stable; they do not have to be trailered in.

Taking the Next Step

Once you've ridden in a schooling show, you should visit an actual show. Your trainer will know about all the different horse shows in your area. You can usually find out more about these shows online. Learn when and where they take place. Find out the different classes that will be competing.

When you go, pick up a program and learn when each event takes place. As you wait, look for the place where the horses will enter. Watch how riders warm up their horses in the ring. Also see if you can spot the different show officials.

Who's Who at the Show

Look around the arena and see who seems to be running things. One of the important people is the show secretary. This person works in an office or booth. He or she checks in all the riders. The secretary gives every rider

Watching and Planning

As you watch the riders and horses perform, pay attention to every little detail. How are the horses and riders turned out? Do the riders seem happy to be there? Is everyone's tack clean? Which riders look confident, organized, and prepared? Which horses look well trained? After the show, do you hear any riders complain about the judge's decisions? Did any of the riders thank the show officials? Try to observe what made some riders seem better than others. Make sure their habits become your habits.

a number, which goes on the rider's back or on the horse's bridle or saddle pad. He or she also makes sure each rider's paperwork is complete.

You will notice a few other officials around the area. One of them is the judge. Small shows might have just one judge, but larger shows have several. Judges stand out in the ring or at a spot where they can watch everything closely. They give scores based on how well the horses and riders perform. They write down the good and bad points of each performance. Finally, they look over the scores and decide who wins first place, second place, and so on.

Another important person is the ring steward or ringmaster. This person keeps the show going smoothly. He or she makes sure the horses are lined up in the right order for each class. The steward directs the riders into the ring and makes sure their numbers are showing. The steward also helps the judges and lets the announcer know what is happening next.

The show announcer is easy to spot. Sitting in a booth with a microphone, the announcer tells everyone what's going on. He or she hears from the judges, secretary, and steward and then makes announcements. This person tells the competitors and crowd which class is coming up next. The announcer tells the riders what the judge wants them to do. He or she also announces changes in the show program.

Deciding to Show

After watching a show or two, you might decide you want to participate. Ask your trainer if you are ready to take this step. Some students catch on quickly, work comfortably with their horses and trainers, ride often, and are ready for a show in only a few months. Others may need more time to prepare. Your trainer can help you decide whether you are ready. He or she can also give you advice about which show to enter and which classes you should compete in.

If you are riding someone else's horse, make sure you have permission to show it. Figure out how to get the horse to the show grounds.

Contact the show secretary to find out how to register. Then sign up, select your classes, and pay the fees.

Choose the clothing you will wear for the show. Whether you compete in western or English riding, make sure everything fits well and looks terrific. Girls should find out how to fix their hair on show day.

The horse's hair is important, too! Find out whether the horses in your class have braided or brushed manes. Ask whether their tails need to be trimmed. Study how to bandage the tail to protect it and to keep it tidy. Keep the horse's coat clean and well groomed.

Continue to practice with your horse. Go through the jumps, gaits, sliding stops, or

It takes a lot of practice before you can compete in a horse show.

other moves that will be required. But don't overdo it. You don't want to bore the horse or wear her out by doing the same maneuvers over and over.

Final Preparations

A few days before the show, make a list of everything you'll need on show day. For instance, you should take a grooming kit, a first-aid kit, and maybe even a friend to help with everything. Your trainer can tell you all of the other things you will need. Also, plan when to get up in the morning, when to eat, when to trailer your horse, and when to leave for the show.

On the day before the show, you will have plenty to do. Make sure your tack is clean and in good shape. If the weather is warm, you might want to wash your horse. You should also lay out your clothes and tack for the next day. As you pack each item, check it off your list.

Five

Show Day

At last! It's time for your first show! By now, all the important decisions have been made. All the paperwork is in. You have practiced and practiced. And today is the big day!

On the morning of the show, it's important to get up early. You want to arrive at the show long before your class competes. You should have a good breakfast—but don't eat anything unusual.

If you are taking your own horse, it's important to feed and water him early. He needs to digest his food before traveling and competing. Give him plenty of time to eat. Then groom him again and braid his mane if it's required.

Also make sure *you* look your best. Your clothing should look clean and sharp. Your boots should not be smudged, and your shirt should be unwrinkled. Girls who compete should have their hair fixed neatly and

← Show day arrives for this rider and her horse!

Dealing with Nerves

Every competitor knows what it's like to be nervous. However, there are ways to deal with this. Right before their class, riders sometimes close their eyes and breathe deeply. They talk softly to their horses. They go through the performance in their minds. Finally, they imagine themselves performing perfectly.

out of the way. Long hair should be in braids, a ponytail, or pinned up under your hat or helmet.

If you plan well, you and your horse will arrive at the show grounds early. Then you can check in at the secretary's booth. You will pick up your number and have someone pin it in place. Check the show's bulletin board for the directions or course diagrams for your classes. If you are in a jumping class, for example, find the map that shows the order of the jumps. Study and memorize all the instructions or maps.

Before you compete, you and your horse should both warm up. Riders often do simple stretching exercises before the show. They also ride their horses around a warm-up ring a few times. They start with a walk, then slowly move up to a trot or canter.

Riders warm up their horses before a dressage competition in Leesburg, Virginia.

You're Up!

Soon, it's time for your class. If you listen to the announcer, you'll know when you're up. You might ride in a flat class first. This is a competition without jumping. All of the riders in the class get ready outside the ring and enter at the announcer's command. The judge watches the riders to see how well they handle their horses. Next, the judge asks the riders to change gaits. As the horses walk, trot, and canter around the ring, the judge keeps track of everyone's performance.

Next, the steward might ask the riders to line up in the center of the ring. The judge walks along the line, makes notes, and checks each rider's number. When the judge is satisfied, he or she hands a scorecard to the steward. The steward takes it to the announcer, who then proclaims the winners. Riders with the top scores usually receive ribbons.

You will probably compete in a few different classes during the day. Before each one, check yourself and your horse to make sure you both still look clean and neat. Remember too, the show is supposed to be *fun*. Keep a pleasant, professional look or

A rider shows her affection for her award-winning horse.

smile on your face. Show everyone that you enjoy what you are doing.

Making New Friends

Always remember that a show is not all business. It's also a great chance to have fun and to make new friends. Very often, riders discover other competitors who live close to them or even go to the same school.

Before a class, riders can keep each other from getting nervous by telling jokes or sharing funny stories. For lunch, everyone in the barn might order pizza. Sometimes shows even offer extra activities such as games or treasure hunts.

Keep a friendly attitude toward the other riders, and congratulate the winners. Always be respectful of the show officials.

At the end of the show, your trainer may ask the judge to comment on your performance. When the judge answers, remember that he or she is trying to help you improve your performance and prepare you for your next show. Thank the judge for the pointers.

Finally, as you clean up and prepare to leave, thank everyone who helped you. Make sure you have the names of the new friends you made that day. Think about what the judge told you and how you will improve. Write it down. Keep a notebook of each show and what you need to work on. After all, another show is coming soon, and you want to be ready!

Glossary

breed   A type of horse.

chariot   A two-wheeled, horse-drawn vehicle that carries one standing person.

cow towns   Small towns in cattle-raising regions.

disciplines   Types of horse training.

endurance riding   A competition that tests a horse and rider's ability to travel long distances.

equestrian   Having to do with horseback riding.

equine   Having to do with horses.

equitation   The art of riding horses.

jousting   A contest in which knights used lances to try to knock one another from their horses.

lances   Long, pole-like weapons with pointed ends.

longeur   A person who guides a horse during vaulting.

obstacles   Things that are in the way and block progress.

reins   Leather straps attached to a horse's bit and used by a rider to control a horse.

steeds   High-spirited horses.

tack   The gear used to outfit a horse.

temperaments   Natural personalities.

Find Out More

Books

Dowdy, Penny. *Cross Country and Endurance*. New York: Crabtree Publishing Company, 2009.

———. *Dressage*. New York: Crabtree Publishing Company, 2009.

Johnson, Robin. *Show Jumping*. New York: Crabtree Publishing Company, 2009.

Kras, Sara Louise. *Horse Riding*. New York: Cavendish Square, 2014.

Loria, Laura. *Show Horses*. New York: Gareth Stevens Publishing, 2011.

Ward, Lesley. *Jumping for Kids*. North Adams, MA: Storey Publishing, 2007.

DVDs

Yeates, B. F. *You and Your Horse*. A seven-DVD series on owning and training a horse.

Zettl, Walter. *A Matter of Trust*. A four-DVD set on training the horse and rider in dressage, 2005.

Websites

Horse Show Central

www.horseshowcentral.com
A site with everything from horse-show listings to a directory of stables in every state.

Fédération Equestre Internationale

www.horsesport.org
The home page of the Fédération Equestre Internationale. This site explains its official disciplines in detail. It also has news about international competitions and winners.

United States Equestrian Federation

www.usef.org
The website of the United States Equestrian Federation, an organization that promotes equestrian sports.

United States Pony Clubs, Inc.

www.ponyclub.org
The home page of the United States Pony Clubs. The site includes information on clubs in each state.

Index

Page numbers in **boldface** are illustrations.

About the Author

Susan H. Gray has a master's degree in zoology. She has taught biology at the college level and has done research on freshwater lakes. She is now a freelance writer and has written more than 120 books for children. Susan especially loves writing about animals. She lives in Cabot, Arkansas, with her husband Michael and many pets.

classes, riders use the kind of **tack**, or equipment, that cowboys use. This includes a large, sturdy saddle with a raised knob called the horn, used in roping. Western riders hold their **reins** in one hand, just like cowboys who need to rope with the other hand. In shows, competitors wear jeans, cowboy

The Rodeo

Is the rodeo a horse show? Not really. Rodeo riders do show how well they and their horses perform. They compete for prizes. But in a rodeo, competitors might also ride enormous bulls, and children might rope goats or ride sheep.

Cowboys developed the rodeo for ranch horses in the 1800s. Back then, cowboys in Mexico, Canada, and the United States went on long,

tiring cattle drives. They drove cattle herds from ranches to **cow towns**, where the cattle were sold. While in town, the cowboys had fun by showing off their riding and roping skills. Over time, these get-togethers became more organized. Today, rodeos are popular mainly in North America. Many cities have junior rodeos just for kids.

boots, chaps, cowboy hats, and color-ful long-sleeved shirts or jackets.

English riding is also popular in many parts of the world. An English-style rider uses a small, light saddle without a horn. This saddle gives the rider more contact with the horse. English riders use both hands to hold the reins. In horse shows, the riders wear tall boots, snug-fitting pants, a solid-color jacket, gloves, a shirt with a white collar and cuffs, and a helmet or top hat.

Shows in Other Countries

Australian shows often include tent-pegging competitions. In tent pegging, riders carry lances and their horses gallop toward pegs in the ground. As the horses pass by, riders jab the pegs with their lances and scoop them up.

Western horse shows are competitions where horses display their response to their rider, their manner, and their disposition.

Sometimes riders miss the pegs completely. Judges give low scores to those riders.

Shows just for Arabian horses are especially popular in the Middle East. In this region of the world, people have raised Arabians for many years. These animals are energetic and sturdy, and they have big lungs. Arabians can withstand long journeys through hot, dry areas. Shows in Saudi Arabia often include rides through the desert to prove how tough the horses are.

English-style riding originated in England. It is a good way to learn how to handle the reins and to control the movement of the horse.